SECULAR HOMESCHOOLER
MAGAZINE

A Home-Learning Community for All

ISSUE ONE

4. MEET THE TEAM

11. WELCOME

12. MAKING ROOM FOR MOUNTAINS BY JAMIE BERG

18. SPEAK PO-ET BY ANWULIKA ANIGBO

22. EBB & FLOW: A HOMESCHOOL MOTHER'S JOURNEY BY JESSICA RIVERA

26. INTRODUCE NATURE JOURNALING TO YOUR HOMESCHOOL BY CHRISTINA LOWRY

32. PEN AND WATERCOLOR LEAF TUTORIAL BY CHRISTINA LOWRY

36. REKINDLE YOUR CHILD-LIKE PASSION FOR LIFE BY E.M. STONE

38. SOCIAL ACTIVISM AND UNSCHOOLING BY ALICIA LUCAS

42. ALONE IN THE WOODS BY MEGAN VAN SIPE

44. 2717 MILES BY JILL HARPER

48. THE BEST HOMESCHOOLING ADVICE I HAVE EVER RECIEVED BY NADINE DYER

54. WHY WE LOVE OUR PARENT PARTNERSHIP PROGRAM BY E.M. STONE

58. CENTER POINT BY MEG NEWLIN

62. HOMESCHOOLING DIGITAL KIDS BY LAUREN BUSFIELD

66. GATHER BY EM BOWERS

70. LEANING INTO THOSE LEARNING SWEET SPOTS BY JESSICA RIVER

74. AT THE BEGINNING BY JAMIE BERG

78. MATH BEYOND WORKSHEETS BY E.M. STONE

84. FINDING PEACE WITH MINIMALISM BY LINDSAY RICE

86. WHY THERE IS NO REQUIRED READING IN OUR HOME BY HEATHER ESTERDAY

90. WHEN DINOSAURS ROAMED THE EARTH BY SHANAN COLVIN

96. HOW TO TALK TO YOUR KIDS ABOUT THEIR GENDER-DIVERSE FRIENDS BY LIV SLAMA

102. HELPFUL LINKS + CREDITS

MEET THE TEAM

E.M. STONE

SH FOUNDER & DESIGNER

Elisabeth created Secular Homeschooler in May of 2017 and has found so much support in the community that has blossomed from it.

She lives in Seattle with her husband and (almost) four children. They're in their third year of homeschooling and have finally discovered that home-education isn't just for kids.

@e.m.stone

LIV SLAMA

ASSISTANT & CONTRIBUTOR

Liv is based in the Pacific Northwest, where she's raising her two kids, herself, and an out-of-control number of houseplants. She writes often about parenting, politics, mental health, and relationships.

facebook.com/livslama
@livslama

NICK STONE

SUBMISSION EDITOR

Nick is a writer and entrepreneur. She divides her passions between the analysis of running a small business and the aesthetics of teaching and writing. She has a Master's degree in literature from the City College of New York and is affiliated with the Jersey City Writers organization.

LINDSAY RICE

CONTRIBUTOR

Lindsay Rice is a wife and homeschooling mom to three children. She has adopted a minimalist lifestyle and it has given her freedom she never thought possible.

@nestedessentials

CHRISTINA LOWRY

CONTRIBUTOR

Christina Lowry never outgrew her childhood love of books, drawing and nature. A tea drinking, handmade loving artist, jeweller and writer, Christina is an unschooling Mama to three. She loves hand knitted cardigans, rainy days and her little people wearing gumboots.

@musing_mama

ALICIA LUCAS

CONTRIBUTOR

Alicia Lucas is an Afro-Latinx and intersectional feminist. She unschools five humans while raising them to be truly free people. They reside in Newark, NJ, and have been on this homeschooling to unschooling journey for five years.

brickcityhomeschool.wordpress.com
@brickcityhomeschool

JESSICA RIVERA

CONTRIBUTOR

Jessica has dabbled in work as a movie theatre employee, airline crew member, teacher, makeup artist, social media manager, and home educator. The list will only continue to grow. She lives with her husband and two children in South Florida.

@theriverafamily

ANWULIKA ANIGBO

CONTRIBUTOR

Anwulika is a Nigerian-American single momma that began homeschooling her now 10-year old son in 2014 after moving to Chicago. She works from home full-time doing development and fundraising for a nonprofit. Anwulika is deeply commited to honoring herself and her son as distinct and autonomous individuals.

@saykedu

NADINE DYER

CONTRIBUTOR

Nadine is a home educating mom to two kids, and hails from northern Ontario Canada. She is a lover of good coffee, good books, and good conversations, and is the author/creator of the blog Up Above The Rowan Tree.

@upabovetherowantree

HEATHER ESTERDAY

CONTRIBUTOR

Heather Esterday homeschools her two sons (ages 7 and 9) in Colorado. In her free time she reads, enjoys board games, and plays violin in a chamber music group comprised of moms.

@colo.mountain.mama

JAMIE BERG

CONTRIBUTOR

Jamie is mom to a little boy and two dogs, wife to a tech dude, and is regaining her identity as a freelancer writer. She actually does love long walks on the beach (or mountain). Originally from the Midwest, she currently lives in the Pacific Northwest.

@bergsinthewild

MEG NEWLIN

CONTRIBUTOR

Meg is a longtime student and teacher of hatha yoga. She is also a wife and a mom, a daughter, a sister and a friend. She lives with her family in the Upper Midwest where she spends most of her days homeschooling her kids, writing, knitting, playing, and trying to convince her family to add more people and pets.

megabenenewlin.com
@treeduckmama

CHRISTINE POWELL DREW

CONTRIBUTOR

Christine is a work-from-home website designer and unschooling mom of two. Books and tea are her love language.

christinepowell.co.za
aloveliveshere.com
@christinepowelldrew

LAUREN BUSFIELD

CONTRIBUTOR

Dr. Lauren Busfield is a clinical social worker and a homeschooling mom of 2 awesome boys. She has been working with adolescents, children, and their families in therapeutic environments since 2008. For the last several years, she has been focusing on ways in which technology impacts the culture of young people.

growingupdigital.org
@lashleighbee

MEGAN VAN SIPE

CONTRIBUTOR

Megan is home educating her two daughters in Michigan, forever finding new ways to live authentically, and always asking deep questions (a classic INFJ move). She writes about her home education journey on her blog School Nest as well as on Instagram.

theschoolnest.com
@schoolnest

EM BOWERS

CONTRIBUTOR

Em is a wife, mama, and home educator living her dream of a simple, small, and slow life in rural Warwickshire, UK.

@simplesmallslow

SHANAN COLVIN

CONTRIBUTOR

Shanan is a music educator turned full-time homeschool mom. She shares her thoughts about homeschooling, parenting and her #boymom adventures on her blog.

@what_we_learned_today

JILL HARPER

CONTRIBUTOR

Jill Harper has been homeschooling her three children since 2003. You can read about her homeschool journey at TAD Town and you can listen to her discuss everything related to homeschooling through her podcast at Podbean.

tadtownhomeschooling.com
simplify4you.podbean.com
@midnightmints

ISSUE ONE | SECULAR HOMESCHOOLER

WELCOME

WE ARE THE NEW GENERATION OF HOMESCHOOLERS

From the beginning, Secular Homeschooler set out to build something new. A reliable resource database for homeschooling families, but we wanted to be more than that. We wanted to make it easier for families to find each other. Our vision for Secular Homeschooler is centered on real science, proven history, and free thought, but just as importantly, community, compassion, and inclusion.

We're here because we believe in the power of truly secular education. When a child is encouraged to approach the world around them with unbounded curiosity, measured skepticism, and unwavering compassion, beautiful things are bound to happen.

This publication is the next step toward building that community. We've worked tirelessly to make it as easy as possible for folks to find the resources they need, which gives them more time to learn and explore alongside their kids. Now, we're ready to hear all about it: the lessons you've learned, the methods you swear by, and the perspectives that are unique to you and your family. Secular education is endlessly valuable, regardless of personal, political, or religious views, and we want to read about how it supplements your family's homeschooling experience.

From one little home-educating family to another, we're thrilled you're here.

MAKING ROOM FOR MOUNTAINS
BY JAMIE BERG

Everyone finds their own path to homeschooling. We all have our own reasons for being here - your kid wasn't thriving in the traditional school atmosphere, the schoolwork wasn't challenging enough, your values didn't align with the system, your family wanted more time to travel, your kid found a passion and wanted the space to explore it. Maybe it was a learning disability, an illness, bullies, tests, homework.

Our family's reason for choosing this path was multifaceted. One of our biggest considerations was giving our son time to explore the world around him. We needed to make room for mountains.

We decided to be intentional about prioritizing nature in our daily time. Our family feels most centered and at peace in the great outdoors. When our son was a baby, and fussed as babies do, we'd step outside and he would quiet himself. He would look up at the trees and the sky, he'd feel the breeze, and he would calm. When he was stroller-bound it was easy to opt outside. Now he's a strong-willed little boy, and sometimes it's a struggle to pull him away from the comfort of pajamas and pretend play in the living room. But we persist, and this is why:

TO BE HEALTHY: Perhaps most pragmatically, there are incredible health benefits to breathing fresh air and stretching our legs. Our hearts, lungs, and our emotional well-being all benefit from time spent moving around in nature.

TO BE CURIOUS: Being outdoors gives us the chance to practice our observational and reasoning skills. Why do you think the tree fell that way? Why is there only snow at the top of the mountain? We fine-tune our senses. We hear birds and bugs, taste berries and salty water, feel moss and stones and sand, smell flowers, and see all that our eyes can take in.

TO BE ADVENTUROUS: Playing outside - running, hiking, splashing, meandering - fosters a love of adventure, an appetite to see and do more. It also teaches us flexibility, patience, and resilience. Plans fall apart, storms pass through, accidents happen. So we stay calm, explore our options, and find a way to adventure on.

TO BE CONNECTED: Being in nature sparks something. We feel connected to something bigger than our small selves, and we feel empowered to take responsibility for protecting our world - a world that will need generations of champions to fix the problems that we've created here for ourselves and our children's children.

TO BE PRESENT: When we're in the mountains (or forests, field, beaches), we let nature set the pace for our days, and our lives take on a calmer, slower, more intentional pace.

TO BE TOGETHER: The shared memories. The bond we create. Enough said.

Homeschooling gives us the time and space to be in this world. We are free to move at a calmer pace, and to be more intentional about how we spend our days. Our son spends less time sitting at a desk and more time out on a trail, moving his body, breathing fresh air. He learns through his experiences and interactions with the natural world, observing and questioning and reasoning. When we come home, we are free to read and draw and watch and continue to stoke our curiosities. He stays curious because he stays an active participant in his learning. He's a driver. Learning is an adventure. He can live what we learn about. And through that, it's my hope that he finds his place and his passion in this world.

If you'd like to find a way to better fit nature into your days, here's how to start:

STEP 1: STEP OUTSIDE

STEP 2: STAY OUTSIDE

Try ten minutes at first. Even on a rainy/cold/humid day, you can find a way to make ten minutes fun. Getting out the door is often the hardest part. As your confidence grows, it will get easier to stay out longer and venture farther. Spell out words with sticks and rocks in your yard. Take a 'listening walk' through the neighborhood. Talk about your day while you're on the trail. Read a book together on a nearby soccer field. Pretend to be explorers. Peruse books and Instagram for inspiration. Join a group. Start a tradition. Get the whole family involved in planning adventures - look at maps together, bake snacks to bring, create something all your own. My family likes to eat peanut butter and jam sandwiches on top of mountains. What about yours?

ORGANIZATIONS TO DISCOVER:

Hike It Baby

Adventure Mamas Initiative

Local Nature Schools (ours has parent-child nature classes that visit a new park each week)

Trail Associations

BOOKS TO CHECK OUT:

There's No Such Thing As Bad Weather by Linda åKeson Mcgurk

Last Child in the Woods by Richard Louv

Vitamin N by Richard Louv

Play the Forest School Way by Jane Worroll and Peter Houghton

How to Raise a Wild Child by Scott D. Sampson

ISSUE ONE | SECULAR HOMESCHOOLER

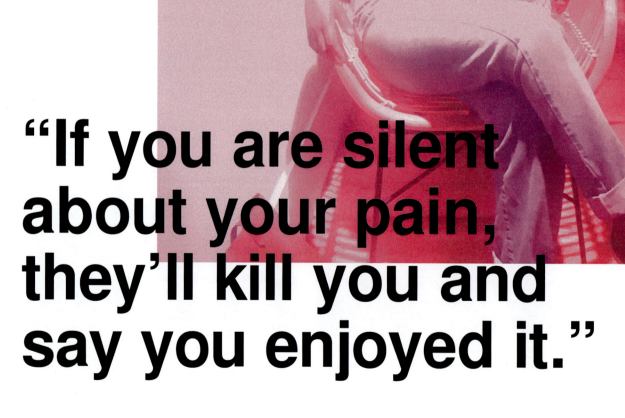

"If you are silent about your pain, they'll kill you and say you enjoyed it."

Zora Neale Hurston

SPEAK PO-ET!
BY ANWULIKA ANIGBO

We live in a culture that does not respect the voice of women and children. We live in a world were the words "child" and "woman" can be used as insults. This doesn't mean we should be quiet. Silence won't bring change - we want because we never had our say.

We also have to speak about our joy and allow our intelligence to be on display. It's vital that we walk around comfortably in our humanity.

We started recording a podcast on my phone because that's what I had. I had mentioned the idea of a podcast months earlier and my son, Afam, seemed uninterested. Then without warning, he asked if we could record the first episode. We sow a lot of seeds in our children and it's impossible to tell what will stick because our eyes can't see below the surface. I wanted to document the things he said - his perspective, his ideas, his experience - for that reason. I was looking at soil that could speak, and I figured listening could give me an idea of what was below the surface.

My son was born the year Obama was elected. He has only ever known a world where Obama or Trump was President. He is living in wildly historic times and I wanted his experience to be documented. I wanted him to know his experience is worth documenting.

ANWULIKA: Why do you think it's important for kids to share their opinions?

AFRAM: I feel like kids should share their opinions because they are real people too with real opinions. We are people and we are part of the society, so our ideas should be valued.

ANWULIKA: What do you think stops kids from sharing their opinions most?

AFRAM: Parents who think that kids should not get an opinion and make all the decisions for their kids.

ANWULIKA: What happens to a person when they don't get to share their opinions?

AFRAM: I think people get mad and they start wanting their opinion to matter more than other peoples.

ANWULIKA: What do you like about hosting a podcast?

AFRAM: I love everything about it. I like the whole thing.

ANWULIKA: Awesome. You listen to podcasts a lot what are some of your favorite podcasts?

AFRAM: Stories Podcast, Brains On, and Dinner Party Downloads.

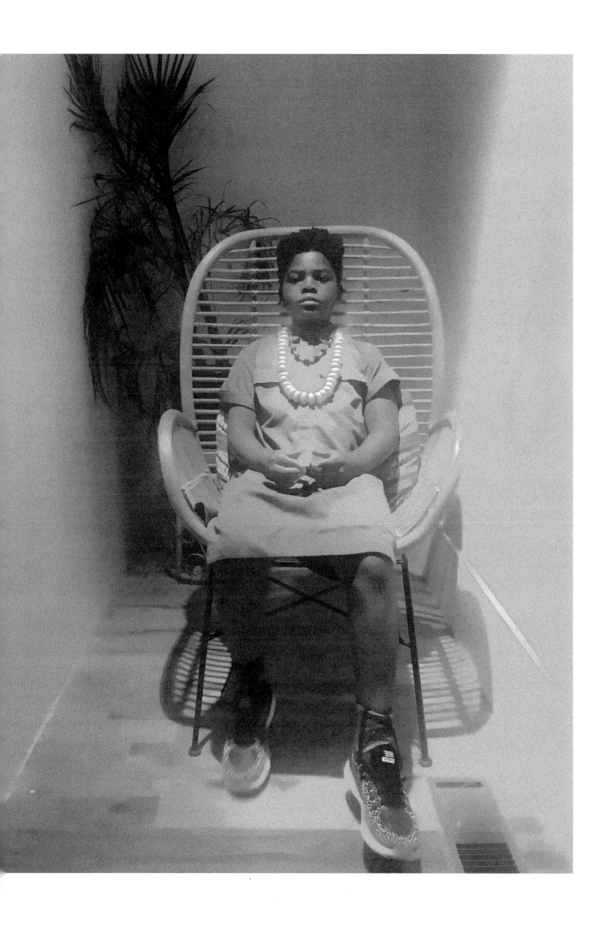

EBB & FLOW: A HOMESCHOOL MOTHER'S JOURNEY

BY JESSICA RIVERA

We often talk about our children's journey with homeschooling. They start off loving it. They ask for more. You join all the homeschool events to fulfill their needs. Then, they start complaining about school work. They resist anything that looks "official". It can work the opposite way too. We homeschool mothers gather together and talk about how our child is reacting to this assignment, how they feel about that curriculum, how they refuse to do math or handwriting or how they love to do art or read all day.

Let's put the topic of our children to the side for a moment. Let us talk about ourselves. Our journey is happening alongside our children's and if there is one thing I've learned, it too goes through an ebb and flow. I can only speak for myself, but maybe you will see just a little bit of your journey in mine.

Once I committed to the fact that I would be homeschooling my children, I became obsessed with learning all I could about homeschooling. I read everything I could get my hands on. I scoured the internet for blogs and stand alone articles. When I felt I had enough information about homeschooling, I started pinning all the amazing lessons on Pinterest. I wanted to do it all with my kids. I have always loved learning new things, and my enthusiasm was obvious. My children were excited and eager. But I was not satisfied. All of a sudden, I found out that there were homeschool accounts on Instagram, and my mind exploded. More information, more knowledge! This led me to learn that there were "types" of homeschooling methods. Well I'll be darned, what were we? Eclectic, Classical, Charlotte Mason, Unschooling. More research. More books. Homeschool podcasts! Say what? Listen for countless hours to learn more about education.

During my pursuit of more homeschool knowledge, I was part of a homeschool group in my area which brought me immense happiness. I joined every single event. I was out four days a week, learning and sharing with these homeschool mothers. We went from unschooling to a secular Charlotte Mason method. It was nearing the end of our third year homeschooling, and then, CRASH! I was burnt out. Too many events. Too many books. Too many podcasts. Too many voices.

I tried to fight it. I didn't want to accept it. I held on for a few more months but it was all for naught. What I didn't know then was that I was simply experiencing an ebb. Just like we do for most other areas of our life, we accept the ebb and flow. We'll pick up a new hobby and a few months later, that hobby will cease, until we pick it up again. And maybe we don't pick up that hobby and that's okay. I watched my son go through a period of being a voracious reader, to not picking up a single book, and then back to reading again.

At the end of our fourth year, I stopped all homeschool. I barely read to my children. I stopped asking my children to read or do any kind of school work. In South Florida, many families lightly homeschool during the summer because of the heat. I also take two months off during the school year to enjoy the weather. My husband noticed that our kids were not doing any school work. I told him I simply lost my joy for homeschooling. It no longer interested me. I did not want to sit with my children to do any kind of learning, even when my children pursued their own interests. If they asked for my help, I flat out did not want any part of it. At first this scared me. The first suggestion made by others was to send them to public school. I found this unfair. Why did I have to be "on" all the time? When my children show a lack of desire, we make room for that feeling and give them time. Couldn't I have the same?

I've been exploring my interests over my childrens'. I am reading more, exercising more, going out with friends more, going out with my husband more, the list continues. I'm not worried about what my kids might not learn because I've given up homeschooling for the moment. I'm not worried that my love for homeschooling has left, because I know that like the push and pull of the tide, it will be back. Homeschooling is the lifestyle for me and for us as a family. In fact, because I am giving myself this break, I find myself missing the fun we had with homeschooling. I can see it coming back slowly. I have set myself free. I don't want to homeschool right now. I don't want to want to plan for the next school year. I don't want to read to my children right now. I don't want to set up paint for them. And I don't feel guilty. The next time you see me, I'll be laughing, knee deep in a science experiment with my kids, living through the ebb and flow of a homeschooling mother.

INTRODUCE NATURE JOURNALING TO YOUR HOMESCHOOL

BY CHRISTINA LOWRY

Children are natural artists and scientists. Their innate curiosity drives their exploration of the world around them. They fill their pockets with treasure, ask a million questions and can scribble their way through an entire scrap book in an afternoon. Nature journaling is a beautiful way to preserve moments of that curiosity and creativity. And it isn't just for children. It encourages adults to see the world through their children's eyes, to shed negative beliefs about their own creativity, to slow down, look closely, and ask 'why'. Together with our children we can record observations and questions, and learn more about the world around us, and ourselves.

Charlotte Mason devotees will be familiar with nature journaling as an essential part of a child's education. However, whatever your homeschooling style, nature journaling offers so much to both child and parent. It is a process of discovery that naturally covers English, Science, Geography, Art, fine motor skills, creativity, and connection with the natural world. In a time when children are reportedly spending less and less time outdoors, nature journaling inspired our family to spend more time exploring in nature, study entomology, keep insects as pets and observe their life cycles first hand.

Nature Journaling is one of my favourite parts of homeschooling. Our approach has evolved over time as I learnt to keep it light hearted and fun. It should never be a chore, but rather inspire a sense of wonder. As unschoolers, our time spent nature journaling is not scheduled, but inspired by our experiences. It is an activity we do together, often as a result of spending time in nature, and it is voluntary. The very act of sitting down and starting to draw in my own nature journal is an invitation my children usually cannot resist.

WHAT EXACTLY IS NATURE JOURNALING AND HOW DO YOU GET STARTED?

It can be equally inspiring and overwhelming to know that Nature Journaling can be nearly anything. Quite simply, it's a sketchbook to draw items found in nature, but it can be so much more. You can make your pages as plain or as decorative as you wish. You can ask questions, include photographs, tape in feathers, pressed flowers and observations. You might include quotes, or poems. You may use pencils, ink, watercolour, crayons, or all of them. There is no right or wrong way, no need to test or mark the contributions to each page. You may journal daily, weekly, or just while travelling. You may choose to sketch only birds, or insects, or landscapes, or a little bit of everything. Each journal is unique.

To get started, let your children choose their own sketchbooks and you choose one too. Gather up pencils and watercolour paints, then take them out to the back yard, a local park or nature trail and invite them to find something they would like to draw. This is the beginning of a process that will bear more and more fruit over time. At first my children drew carton figures of animals, and with gentle encouragement, write the date and the name of the animal. Over the past year my children have gradually taken more and more pride in their work, their interest has been piqued by many topics and they are now recognising species, taking note of seasonal differences, copying life cycle diagrams, and committing small details to paper.

Every moment you spend outside, every nature documentary, every book that celebrates the natural world will excite in them the possibilities of nature and with time and encouragement you will be amazed at the way your children respond to the world around them.

Those blank journals are full of possibilities!

NATURE JOURNALING IDEAS & ACTIVITIES

[01] Leaf rubbing

[02] Mushroom prints

[03] Nature scavenger hunt

[04] Bees wax dipped leaves

CHRISTINA'S FAVORITE SUPPLIES

[01] Micron waterproof pens in black sizes 0.1 and 0.05

[02] 2B pencils

[03] Stacking water colour palettes

[04] Ranger Dylusions Creative Journal

PEN AND WATERCOLOR LEAF TUTORIAL

BY CHRISTINA LOWRY

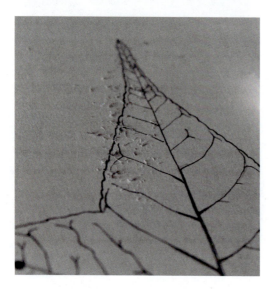

If you are new to nature journaling, leaves are a great place to start. Even if you think you are a terrible artist, just a few simple lines makes for a recognisable leaf. Plus, you can cheat! Choose a leaf that catches your eye, lay it on your sheet of paper and trace around it with an HB pencil. That gets the tricky part out of the way.

Now is the time to really delve into the purpose of nature journaling, to look closely at your leaf and see all the details you wouldn't ordinarily notice. But don't become overwhelmed by every single vein and texture. Just because you see all the detail doesn't mean you need to include it all. I chose to sketch in the main veins in my leaf and hint at the others. Once you are happy with your details, go over your pencil work with a waterproof fine black pen. I use a 0.05mm Micron or Staedtler for this. Then erase your pencil lines.

Cut a little strip of paper out of the back of your sketchbook to test your paint colours. Whether you are mixing colours or using them straight from the pan, it is handy to be able to test the colours beforehand and know exactly what they will look like on your paper. Look for the darker and lighter areas of your leaf and start blocking them in. Then use a smaller brush to add detail and dab in the discolouration on the leaf.

In no time you will have a beautiful leaf in your nature journal. If it didn't turn out as perfectly as you imagined just toss the actual leaf back out in the garden! This is your starting point. Add the date, write a few observations about the weather, what your children are interested in, what birds you are seeing, what time sunrise and sunset are. You will cherish all of these little details as you look back on your nature journal in times to come.

Formosan Gum
liquidambar formosana

REKINDLE YOUR CHILD-LIKE PASSION FOR LIFE

BY E.M. STONE

+Watch inspiring movies that remind you of the joy and creativity of childhood. My personal favorites are Hook and Matilda.

+Read a childhood classic such as Charlie and the Chocolate Factory.

+Do an art project with your child. Messy is good. Take it further and build a mud pie or sand castle.

+Do an art project *without* your child. Get completely lost in the process.

+Play a game that you loved as a kid. Get competetive and make it fun.

+What do you want to learn? Buy curriculum for yourself and study alongside your child. Do a project for your own educational growth.

+Binge-listen to the tunes you loved in your early teen years.

+Take your kids to the skating rink and join them while humming or singing along to the music.

+As a child, you woke early because you were excited about life. Find a way to look forward to morning time.

+Look through your old photo albums. Do you remember the way you felt in the images? Do you remember why?

"Anyone with artistic ambitions is always trying to reconnect with the way they saw things as a child."

Tim Burton

SOCIAL ACTIVISM & UNSCHOOLING
BY ALICIA LUCAS

When I was invited to submit to this issue of Secular Homeschooler I was surprised, excited, and amped to get started on my piece. I was asked to write about how we as an unschooling family work social activism into our unschooling, and how is it that we work on raising our children to be the next generation of activists. I had no earthly idea how to start this off, though. For us our social activism is an organic part of who we are and not something that we consciously incorporated. Social activism is imperative to building a better world for us and our community. As an Afro-Latinx family with children who are part of the LGBTQIA community, social activism is something we must be a part of, it is essential to securing a safe place in this world, especially in the current political environment, in which racism and bigotry have been given new life.

For our family social activism and fighting for social justice comes in many forms. The most recognizable form is attending rallies and marches for causes we find important, and that speak out against injustices. We have done this on a regular basis as a family for the past five years. However, our integration of talking about and modeling the way of social activism started before our first march as a family, and before we began our unschooling journey.

We were always honest and forthright with our children when it comes to discussing difficult things. While it's important to do the obvious things—teaching them history in an honest and accurate way, discussing the importance of voting, especially in local elections, and taking them to vote—these are not the ways we raise social activists. Rather, teaching social activism is embedded in everything we do.

Our family is all about raising liberated humans. We do our best to hold space so that they feel safe in voicing themselves when it comes to body autonomy, and unapologetically taking up physical space in the world. We do not expect our children to give us hugs, kisses, on demand, nor do we demand they give up their body autonomy just to please others, including friends or family. We accept all people for who they are, not just our children. However we also do our best to show our children that accepting people as they are does not come at the expense of one's physical and mental well being. Trust me when I say raising our children in this way is a revolutionary act. Having, Afro-Latinx children, walking in the world demanding respect, and demanding to be treated like fully formed human beings is a huge form of social activism. It is what will make them ready to be leaders, and activists in their community. This is no small feat.

Aside from the work we do as a family on a personal level, we also contribute to building our community. As BIPOC (Black, Indigenous, and People of Color) unschoolers who are also about raising free people and fostering intersectionality, cultivating an environment in our neighborhoods is a big part of our social activism. Clearly, as homeschoolers/unschoolers we all have sat in our homes and thought, I wish there was (fill in the blank) available for homeschoolers/unschoolers like us. Here is the thing as the fine folk at Secular Homeschooler have modeled for us: we can and should be those people.

For me this aspect of our social activism began with my wish for some sort of STEAM (science, technology, engineering, arts and math) exhibition for homeschoolers/unschoolers, that was just a showcase and was not segregated by age. That was when that light bulb came on and I made that very event happen, and I am currently planning for another one this year. I also was welcomed to collaborate on a Homeschoolors of Color Collective day where myself and two other BIPOC homeschooling/unschooling families organized a day of sharing our experiences and knowledge with other parents who were curious about or new to homeschooling and looking for ideas and resources. It was so well received that we are planning another one.

Since these were events that had a direct impact on my children, I asked them to take an active role in being a part of organizing and participating in both these events, and they were given the room to participate as much or as little as they wanted. I tell this because by modeling these actions, and taking initiatives when we see something missing in our communities, in working on filling those needs ourselves and instead of waiting for someone else to do it we instill in our children that they can make the changes in their communities themselves. They do not have to wait for someone else to take the reins, and activism doesn't have to be in the form of huge gestures.

The last bit I will leave you with is, give your child(ren) the space to figure out what they are passionate about, how they want to better, their home, community, city, etc. and let them lead the way in how they feel is best to be activists. Activism about doing the work, there is no small such thing as small movements, all big movements start small, with one person or one family. Now let's go forth and change the world.

ALONE IN THE WOODS
BY MEGAN VAN SIPE

There's a sand-covered park at the edge of our small Michigan town that's tucked into the woods on a dusty side road. We stumbled upon it one day by accident, after living in this town for three years. While playing there one humid day in July, I noticed what looked like the entrance to a trail - a small opening in the thick ferns.

"Hey, guys! Come here! I think I found a trail. Should we explore?" I called to my sandy, sweaty wildlings.

They ran after me and grabbed my hands as we stepped into a new world of thick woodland wonder. We found bright red mushrooms, ghostly Indian Pipe, wild strawberry plants creeping along the edge of the path, and ferns as far as we could see. We went back again and again until it became ours. The woods had been there all that time with her arms outstretched, waiting for us.

We spent the past year, our first year as homeschoolers
going to the woods alone to discover, wonder, climb
and listen. This has enriched us beyond anything
could have expected when we first stepped foot onto
the trail. In the center of the web of intersecting
trails, there's a fallen log that has been carved into
a bench. When we came upon the bench on that
first hike, the three of us climbed onto its damp
surface and sat in silence, in awe of the magic
around us. There are some things that are ever
better when experienced alone, with space to just be

The decision to educate our kids at home is like
stepping into the fern-filled woods. It is enriching
curious, enticing, exciting, scary, and beautiful. I
isn't crowded here. We are often alone in these woods

Without the structured community of an organized
school, or the like-minded community some get from
their faith, we are on our own moss-carpeted path. We
have the space to listen to our intuitions and follow ou
interests. We have the time to try new things and switch
gears based on the needs of our families. We have the
empowerment to learn to navigate an unconventiona
life and enjoy the bountiful fruits of that labor

It takes a certain level of scrappiness to gear up fo
this journey. We have to be brave and confident ir
our steps forward without the guidance of a crowc
we can follow. We need our first aid kit, filled with
the encouragement of others on the path up head
We need to pull our fellow hikers up and invite
them to join us if we find them sitting somewhere
along the way. Our community is out there, and we
are alone together in the beautiful, mystical woods

2,717 MILES
BY JILL HARPER

It is a beautiful and cool summer evening. The sun has just set and a breeze is blowing through my open window. This is California weather and I love it. Warm and sunny during the day, but come evening it always cools down. I sit here wondering if the weather in New York is cool at night. Perhaps it is humid and hot. I really don't know.

In fact I have thought very little about New York over the years. I went there once when I was quite young and the only thing I remember is driving by the Statue of Liberty. I pause in my thoughts wishing I knew more, hating that I am even contemplating my lack of knowledge. And what is the force behind my new obsession with New York? My son, my oldest child, is turning my thoughts there.

My son, Truffaut, will be starting college in New York this fall. In fact in less than a week he and I and his little brother will be packing the car full of his most prized possessions and driving him across the country to get there. I will be leaving behind his twin sister Autry who is in summer school at her own college here in California. She goes to school nearby and still lives at home. She started a year before her brother and the transition was seamless. No tears, no hard goodbyes.

Truffaut had other plans, a different path. These two were never afraid to take separate paths from each other. My son has been homeschooled from the beginning. My daughter homeschooled most of the time but also went to public school for a couple grades throughout the years. My daughter is a gifted musician, my son a quiet thinker. My daughter decided to stay close to home for college to save money. My son felt he had to go far away so he could make the transition to adulthood easier.

Sometimes when they were quite little and we were just starting on our homeschool journey, I would wonder where it would all end. Would we make it through the elementary years, the middle school years, the high school years? Would I be able to homeschool them all the way through? I was young and a little naive and because of this I was confident in my ability to do just that. We officially started homeschooling when the twins were four, and we did make it through to the very end.

Truffaut and his sister Autry exceled under homeschooling and it became a way of life for us. When we started, the secular community was smaller, the offerings much more limited, but it worked. And my twins, the ones who were born early and had some difficulties, were not held back by any of that at home. Homeschooling allowed them to progress at their own rate, to work on their strengths and struggles as needed, and to follow passions. And it allowed my daughter to go to college at eighteen and my son to wait an extra year because he knew he needed a little more time.

And homeschooling gave me so much. I had more time with my children than I ever imagined I would get. More cuddles on the couch, more time to read books, more time for walks outside, more time for building Legos, more time to teach essays, and more time just being with them, learning with them, and enjoying them when they were young and through the teenage years.

This wonderful time is now coming to an end and I find myself in tears quite often. I am so proud of Truffaut: Proud to see all his hard work pay off, proud of the man he has become, proud that he is strong enough to move to a state he has never been to, proud that he is doing all this as a person with a disability. His strength amazes me.

And so I sit here tonight thankful for homeschooling, for the time I had because of it, for the young adults that were shaped by it. Just as my son has the courage to move 2,717 miles across the country, I will have the courage to drop him off at his dorm, the courage to say goodbye, and the courage to get back into the car for the drive home to California without him.

THE BEST HOMESCHOOLING ADVICE I HAVE EVER RECEIVED

BY NADINE DYER

Not very long ago in my homeschooling life, I was lucky enough to receive what turned out to be the best homeschooling advice I have ever been given.

It wasn't regarding The Perfect Curriculum, or the Perfect Homeschooling Method, or The Greatest Homeschool Philosophy. It was something else entirely.

I had been really struggling, as a secular Charlotte Mason-inspired home educator, to find my place in the homeschool world. I knew it was possible to have a secular, joyful, and wonderful Charlotte Mason homeschool. The people around me didn't necessarily agree. Every blog post I read on this approach to education, every article, every book, every Facebook group I was a part of - they all made me feel like I was doing it wrong. It really came to a point where I felt so dejected, confused, and wrong, that I nearly gave up homeschooling altogether.

I reached out to someone who had always given great, encouraging wisdom. This person was Leah Boden (of Modern Miss Mason) - she herself is not secular, but a woman of faith. However, no one has been more supportive and more encouraging of my crafting my own path within this educational philosophy. She's a cheerleader for all homeschool parents, and she said something to me that I will carry with me for all my homeschool days.

When I reached out to her with a broken heart, feeling stressed and overwhelmed, Leah said to me: "Nadine, you know what you're doing. You know what your children need. You are the best mother for your children. Tune out all of the other voices around you - block them out, mute the FB groups, unfollow some blogs, put a safe boundary around you and you'll know what you need to do."

"TUNE OUT ALL THE VOICES AROUND YOU."

One simple phrase that turned out to be one of the most profound pieces of advice I could have been given.

We, as home educating parents, are being constantly bombarded by "homeschool celebrities" and their advice and how-to's. If you take a glance on Pinterest, you'll see pin after pin with titles like "the 5 Best Ways to..." and "Follow this advice to your best homeschool ever". All well meaning - as the author of a blog myself, I know that when we write these articles they are given and written with the best of intentions.

Eventually though, they become too much. All of these voices turn into a mess of buzzing and totally overwhelm our minds and hearts. We become so inspired by some of these voices and personalities, that we forget the truest thing about home education: we are the ones who know our child best. We are the perfect parents for our child. We are the leaders of our own homeschools.

It can be a good thing to be able to do a quick search and find an article or blog post or video, on something we're struggling with or a curriculum choice we need to make. All of the information out there now about home education, all of the groups that are often tailored to a particular way of home educating, they're all a good and useful tool for us on our journeys. We just have to remain very conscious of using them as tools and not as Absolute Truth, or as shackles to tie us down.

We have to remember, these big homeschool personalities are just home educating parents like us. They're human, they struggle, and they do not have all the answers. It can be really easy to put them on a pedestal and think "this person says this curriculum is no good, I shouldn't use it". We give their opinions more weight than we give our own!

This time of year, as I'm fine-tuning our plans and making my last minute decisions, I now go inward. I close myself and my heart off from a lot of online groups and blogs that I follow. I circle the wagons, and make a protective boundary around my homeschool. I do this deliberately and consciously. If a particular group makes me feel like I'm not doing enough, or doing it the right way, it goes on mute. If a particular blog's posts tend to make me want to second guess myself or do something radically different, I silence them for a while. In fact, this year, I've muted just about every homeschool FB group I am a part of, and have unfollowed quite a few blogs and websites.

I go to my own heart and I spend time contemplating and observing my children as they are. I look at my family and our interests and habits and values and priorities. I do this with clear eyes, and a quiet mind. I tune out all of the extraneous voices and opinions. And I remind myself that I am the best parent for my child, I know their hearts and their hurts and their passions and their struggles unlike any other single person on this planet. I don't need any "homeschool expert" to tell me what to do, because I already know.

Eventually, when I'm feeling confident and secure in my own mind and my own thoughts, I start to let some voices filter in through the bubble. I realize that there are a few homeschool celebs whose voices and thoughts I appreciate. There are people who encourage me, and make me feel competent and supported. Those people, they get to come back into my blanket fort. And the ones who consistently make me feel like I'm doing it wrong, or don't know what I'm doing - they tend to be kept just outside the bubble.

I'm learning, slowly but surely, how important it really is to keep this protective space around my heart as a home educating parent. Your heart is a sacred space, your mind is wise, and you need to protect them.

WHY WE LOVE OUR PARENT PARTERNSHIP PROGRAM

BY E.M. STONE

If you've never heard of a parent partnership program, think public school but for homeschoolers. I had always joked with my now-husband when we were younger about longing for a place where homeschoolers to go meet up and do school. He would laugh and say, "You mean school?" No.

We began homeschooling a few years ago and discovered just a place like this. To say I'm obsessed is an understatement. A lot of states offer programs like this. This one was started by a few motivated parents!

HERE ARE 8 REASONS WE LOVE OUR PARENT PARTNER PROGRAM:

[01] **IT'S SCHOOL FOR HOMESCHOOLERS, BUT COOLER.** When we first visited this place it looked just like a regular school. There was a parking lot, school buses, lockers, classrooms, teachers with badges, and a cafeteria. I had a bad feeling because I didn't want to replicate public school. It turns out it simply utilizes all the amazing things that are to love about traditional public school while putting total control and independence into the hands of the participating families.

[02] **A SINGLE BUILDING TO RULE THEM ALL.** This one building is where my children will begin "preschool" and it is also where they will graduate "high school" in many years. They will maintain friendships with the same kids they've been hanging out with since they were five, instead of being separated to go to a different junior high or high school building. My youngest ones will have eighteen years of memories in these hallways. Many of the workshops are bundled together with children of all ages. My 6-year-old is not intimidated by 15-year-olds because it is normal to be around each other during the day. The older children help out with the younger children as though we live in some kind of utopian learning village.

[03] **WE MAINTAIN ALL THE EXCITING TRADITIONS AND ROUTINES OF PUBLIC SCHOOL.** We have school dances, science fairs, musicals, talent shows, and spelling bees. We have a first day of school and a last day of school. We have winter, spring, and summer breaks. We leave 2nd grade and we enter 3rd grade. Yes, we're still hanging out with all other ages and seeing many of the same teachers BUT GUESS WHAT? We're in the 3rd grade section of the yearbook because we also had school photos done in October. Not alternative "homeschool" photos - real, classic, traditional, always awkward Lifetouch photos. Our program requires parents to get them done as well. At first I hated it but now I kind of love getting to be involved in these traditions alongside my kids.

[04] **TEACHERS AND STUDENTS ARE EQUALLY ALIVE AND INSPIRED.** Your child picks which classes they want to attend. Each class is taught by a different and dedicated teacher that is passionate about their subject. Children walk in excited to be in the course that they chose and they walk out refreshed because they just studied with a classroom full of kids that are all as motivated as they are.

[05] **WE GET A HELPFUL CHUNK OF MONEY EACH SCHOOL YEAR FOR HOMESCHOOLING COSTS.** You read that right. Now the catch? You won't want to use it to buy curriculum, even though you could. We use 100% of our budget to pay for workshops like ballet or karate. Maybe a few bucks here and there for consumable workbooks. Any curriculum we need for outside of classes, I either buy from our personal money or I check out for the school year from the fully-stocked resource library.

[06] **ARBITRARY RULES ARE PROVEN UNNECESSARY.** Kids are allowed to walk out and use the bathroom as needed. They're allowed headphones and gum and phones and computers. There are no ridiculous rules against tank top straps or colorful hair.

[07] **ADULTS GET TO ADULT.** Parents can get work done, have quiet time, or socialize and make real adult friends during the hours spent at the center. I've made a few. Some of them have kids that don't even hang out with my kids. Those are the best kind of adult friends. Where are those kids anyways? Probably running around the gym with their friends.

[08] **KIDS GET TO HAVE A REAL VOICE.** My daughter is obsessed with history. She didn't get it from me, I've been living in fairy tales since I was old enough to read. She wants the world to be as excited by history as she is and she wants to learn from what other people are passionate about. She asked me one day, "Why do we have a science fair but not a history fair?" I told her to go start one. So she did. That easy. Now she gets to organize and launch this amazing new project for the community and thus begins her own personal legacy within the program. Every single kid gets to have a voice and say in this community. Every single one of them can contribute as they wish and make it a more robust place for everyone.

CENTER POINT

BY MEG NEWLIN

I'm not sure how it is for most families, but ours has always moved around what I have come to think of as the center point. It is the pause between cycles, the brief moment that lies just after the end of one year and right before the start of the next. It is our family's big exhale, a few slow beats before our next in-breath. The center point of our year generally occupies several weeks in the middle of summer when we retreat from our daily lives to our small family home on an island in coastal Maine.

It is pretty ideal. And after the last decade or so, time on the island has become one of recalibrating and reorganizing for each of, both on our own and as a collective. I get enough distance here, when we are truly off at sea, to look back on the year prior with a bit more honesty and perspective than I could afford to when I was in the thick of it. I attempt to get right with myself, take a somewhat more detached look at where I succeeded and where I fell short.

Then I endeavor to let it go. To give myself permission, as well as a hefty hug of inspiration, to begin again. It is my challenge, as a homeschool mama, to tease out the truth of our children from the tangle of my own agenda. There are, of course, the things that I want to learn, and how I think we ought best to learn them. Don't we all want to be exploring history in a linear fashion as well as using composition as a means for illustrating connections past and present? I mean, doesn't that sound great? And make tons of sense? And well, then there is the truth of my two very different and unique kids. Not only unique from me, but markedly distinct from one another. Which means that the opportunity of our home school is founded on my ability and willingness to really see them and teach to them in ways that honors their differences, preferences, interests and desires.

I have the rather unfortunate (amazing!) tendency to jump enthusiastically into anything my kids show the remotest degree of interest in and proceed to assault them with a tremendous amount of ideas, suggestions, resources until I pretty much kill it right there on the spot. Some of this is my own thrill. I love to be a learner and a teacher. But there is also the fear and doubt that this path of home education is going to fail them, fail me, and once and for all reveal me as the fraud that I have always feared myself to be. Worse than all of that, the fear and doubt blinds me from seeing them.

One Monday evening, late last winter, I was heading out to teach one of my weekly classes in town- for which I am gone 3 hours all told. Maple had forestalled the work that I had been pestering her to complete for much of the day and I let her know- in all of my most serious tones- that it had certainly better be complete by the time I returned home- and yes, yes, mom of course stop nagging me and don't you think I know what my work is?!? Ahem. Well, I am sure it hardly bears mentioning but of course 3 hours later when I got back she hadn't touched a single thing. It's a familiar story. Between the sorry, I forgot and my own blind frustration at our obvious (to me!) failure I was almost (so close!) oblivious to what she HAD been doing for all that time.

While I was working, she had been sitting in her room listening to episodes from "Missed in History", a history buff's podcast, while experimenting with color work in a knit bag that she had recently begun with her handwork group. I mean, he was doing it! She was living into her own curiosity and desire and leaning into exactly what child led learning means! I almost missed it, just barely.

So, during this pause at the center point on the island of my family's year, I reorient myself to myself. I remember what it is to see my children clearly and not let my fear compromise my vision. I use this time to plot a path for the year ahead that recognizes the individual. A path that outlines as much space (often a lot) and structure (sometimes more than others) as is needed for both kids. And then I do whatever it takes to my own tendencies, agenda, schedule, so that I may have my best chance of keeping my eyes open to the truth of these growing, changing, shifting, dynamic, magical, humans.

ISSUE ONE | SECULAR HOMESCHOOLER

HOMESCHOOLING DIGITAL KIDS
BY LAUREN BUSFIELD

Access to technology is one of the greatest gifts that we as educators can give our young people. Despite our fear culture warning us daily of technological advances and their dangerous implications, we have so much to gain from our relationship with the digital world. To some of us, this seems intuitive—but the research and the writing leans heavily towards warnings, preventatives and safeguards, rather than the vast array of experiences that are opened up to our children to help them grow in a digital world. In my professional and academic work, I've focused on technology and mental health impacts, but with the underlying idea that distrust of new technologies is an old societal habit, and that young people coming of age in the digital world need to be respected as experts on their experiences, rather than heavily regulated and restricted due to the hesitations of their parents. I've proposed focus on the mindful consumption of digital media, and created tools to help families better manage their digital lives. But how does homeschooling intersect additionally with technology in our everyday lives?

Homeschoolers have more opportunity to engage with technology, but perhaps are also at risk of over-indulgence more than their peers because of that opportunity. It's often tempting to outsource to our digital resources when we're burned out, or when our young students just seem to pay more attention when information is coming from a screen. Once we do that, we sometimes question our motivations for its use, our dedication to our book-heavy, hands-on learning environments, and maybe even question our abilities as educators because of the negative narrative our society plays about screens.

As homeschooling parents, especially the secular variety, we say we love STEM. We love science and technology, and we encourage our kids in their pursuit of tech skills-acquisition. Tech is great…right? But instead of having more conversations about the amazing video game worlds that our little humans create, we worry that they are spending so much time on that game. We want them to be social, but question if social media is the right place to do it. If you're like most parents, you spend more time cautioning, warning, 'turn-it-off'-ing than you do focusing on the opportunities kids are grasping in the digital world. So do I propose you let the kids spend 10 hours a day on video games and talk indiscriminately to everyone online? Of course not. But I do propose we change the conversations that we're having from worried restrictions to positive opportunity-seeking.

In psychology and some business circles, there's an often-used, never-cited saying that it takes about ten positive interactions to outweigh each negative one. The goal for parents interacting with their kids is never that there will be no negative conflict—rather, that the scales are heavily tipped towards the positive. Let's try applying that to our lives with technology and kids. Let's embrace the good, and accept that there will also be some bad, some scary, some uncertainty. Accept the negativity without dwelling in it; if we can do that, we open doors for ourselves and for our kids, and invite in a new world of endless possibilities.

USE THE 'TECHTIVITIES' FOUND HERE AS A JUMPING-OFF POINT TO FOSTER POSITIVE EXPERIENCES WITH TECH--YOU CAN DOWNLOAD THIS AS A BOOKMARK AND FIND OTHER PRINTABLE RESOURCES FOR TECH AND FAMILY LIFE AT GROWINGUPDIGITAL.ORG.

Techtivities

 look for the coolest explosion video you can find on YouTube

 explore the meaning of one word you've never heard or used before

 add two books released this year to your wishlist-- read the reviews!

 write a conversation to each other: using only emojis

 play a coding game, together

 find a new tech skill to learn together, like design, 3D printing, photo-editing or video-making

"Encouraging Our Children to Collect Brings Joy, Passion, and Connection"

GATHER
BY EM BOWERS

I will never forget the delight that accompanied the discovery of our first skull. It was a bright autumn day with clear blue skies overhead and cracking leaves underfoot. We could all sense the coming of winter in the chilled air. We had spent the afternoon exploring a dearly loved woodland near our home, that had become the ever welcoming host to one of our weekly nature walks. On this particular day, we had jolly intentions of searching for owl pellets. We were all keen to find one as this particular treasure from nature had eluded us.

As we began to gently run our fingers through the fallen leaves surrounding the bases of the trees we thought might have made good owl feeding territory, my 5 year old decided to explore the bank upon which a badger sett had aroused his curiosity. And then he saw it – a hint of bone just visible through the golden leaf litter. He knew what it was immediately, and the sheer joy of his find filled our hearts with wonder and awe. An old, clean, sun bleached, beautiful and intact badger skull was laying on the earth beneath our feet.

Watching my son, seeing his vibrant outward display of childlike delight and enchantment at such a find, I also knew that there was a much deeper, personal sense of intrigue and connection that would now guide him along a journey of understanding. To be a gatherer does not only involve "collecting stuff" – he tells me that often. For us, it also means we are a part of a beautiful, changing, evolving, complicated world and we seek to understand not just by collecting and displaying the treasures that we find, but by embarking on our own personal journeys of discovery.

These journeys began when the children were very small – pockets filled with pebbles and acorns, pine needles, feathers, and sticks. For children, there seems to be deep need to gather, to collect. It is as if by doing so, they are part of nature, at one with the world, connected to all life and the history of our time. Each one of these objects is important and special in a way that only the child can understand. I know first hand of the distress, of both mother and child, when a beloved rock is misplaced or a shell is left on a bench.

A old wooden bowl served as our very first gathering space as we needed somewhere to empty the pockets into. Little by little, another bowl for leaves was added, then a tray with fossils, a glass jar filled with seaglass and pebbles from a coast walk, a wooden box with insects. The children began to ask for shelves and containers as birthday gifts and they were fortunate to be given a beautiful wooden and glass display cabinet to house their most special discoveries. Marine mammal bones found on a wild Irish beach, empty and cracked bird egg shells whose occupants had long since taken to the skies, sun-bleached seabird skeletons and delicate butterflies are safe from dust here, and can be brought out at any time to touch, sense, understand and respect.

As our curious collection of gatherings grew, they started to become less curious and more understood as the journeys of discovery advanced. And it is not only the unusual and rare pieces of natural history, such as the badger skull or the wasps nests, that have been the most precious. A found blackbird feather wasn't just a feather. It symbolised the door to a world of birds that they excitedly began to explore. They wanted to know more and more about blackbirds. They read about them, drew them in their nature journals and we all learnt to birdwatch with our eyes open and closed. We discovered how many pairs were nesting in the trees and hedges that bordered our garden. They watched them feeding at the bird table in the snow, and recognised their alarm calls all through the warmer spring days.

As we began to feel closer to the blackbird, other birds caught our attention too. Seeing blue tits, song thrushes, wrens, fieldfares, redwings, bullfinches and robins became part of our days, with us living alongside them, recognising their behaviours and habits. Birdwatching became a passion for the children. Their found feathers from all manner of birds now take pride of place upon our cabinet, each one linking the owners and our children in a vital, passionate and life affirming web of life. Gathering the blackbird feather on a muddy country lane was just the beginning.

Encouraging the children to gather, to collect and to discover has been a integral part of our home education journey. We gather from nature using discretion, respect and responsibility, following countryside guidelines and laws for collectors and naturalists in our area. So many children now are told not to touch nature, in effect living apart from their world, and are missing the joy of discovery and the deep feelings of peace that come from acknowledging that we are not separate from nature, but a part of it. Wonderful and inspiring naturalists such as Sir David Attenborough and the late Gerald Durrell are our mentors – encouraging young naturalists to engage, question, learn and marvel. As a mother, to watch them connect with the natural world with such wonder and awe through being curators of their own museums has been a captivating and humbling journey.

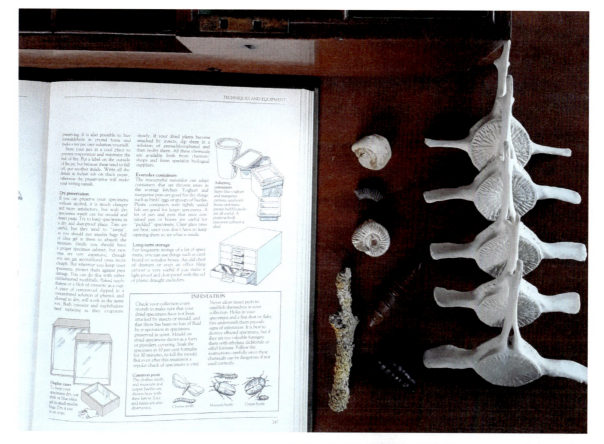

BOOK & AUDIO SUGGESTIONS

The Amateur Naturalist by Gerald Durrell

Cabinet of Curiosities by Gordon Grice

Last Child in the Woods by Richard Louv

Life Stories by Sir David Attenborough

SETTLING INTO THOSE LEARNING SWEET SPOTS

BY CHRISTINE POWELL DREW

Back when I was a very new mom, I remember wanting to teach my son ALL THE THINGS. I tried to teach him baby sign language, elimination communication, and researched games to play with babies to encourage early motor skills. I now laugh at how enthusiastic I was. I was soon cured of this with my son doing everything in his own damn time, including saying his first words.

At 18 months old he could not say more than two words and I was contemplating speech therapy. Six months later he was speaking in full sentences and had an advanced vocabulary for his age. I am so glad I didn't resort to speech therapy -- he clearly just needed a bit more time and I often think that speech therapy may have bumped him off his unique learning path and perhaps caused issues down the line.

I mellowed into this new found 'leave him to get there in his own time' approach and was completely surprised when at three years old he had taught himself all the colours. I certainly hadn't taught him! We did read a lot of books and he would ask what colours were whenever he needed to know. He found it enthralling that colours had names, a code he had to crack, and he was determined to do so. He enlisted everyone he spent time with much to the frustration of his colour blind grandfather to NAME ALL THE COLOURS!

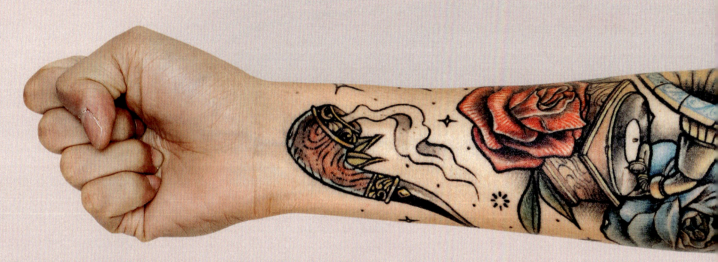

I didn't realise it then but he had entered his colour learning sweet spot. I couldn't stop him from learning if I had tried.

True to form, he completely blew me away when, at age 5, he sorted all of our vintage encyclopedias in numerical order. Honestly, I hadn't even realised he knew all of the numbers, let alone their order. We had at that stage decided to following an unschooling approach to learning and I was super relaxed about it all because he was still so young. He spent most of his days outside playing with the dogs and climbing trees so where did he learn to count to twelve, to recognise the numbers and know how to place them in sequential order?

It was only after this that I took note of how interested in numbers he really was. He had been prompting me to teach him all about addition, subtraction, even multiplication and division just by asking tons of questions (as he always does). By answering to his inquiring mind he learned what he had decided he needed to know.

It was only after this that I took note of how interested in numbers he really was. He had been prompting me to teach him all about addition, subtraction, even multiplication and division just by asking tons of questions (as he always does). By answering to his inquiring mind he learned what he had decided he needed to know.

ISSUE ONE | SECULAR HOMESCHOOLER

My son is now 7, almost 8, and he cannot read. Not even a little. To say I am completely relaxed about this fact would be a lie as I am a dedicated reader myself, but I think I'm more chilled than most. We are almost sure that we will continue with an unschooling approach to education as this seems to be best for my son and our family. Up until now we have had time on our side as he hasn't ever really fallen 'behind' his peers, even those who attended academic preschools. However, at 7, almost 8 and not being able to read he is now 'behind'.

I guess it takes courage and trust in your child and their learning process to leave your child to be 'behind'. If I had not already seen the evidence myself on just how successful leaving him to learn things on his own terms was, I would surely have caved by now and brought out the flash cards.

And how do unschoolers learn to read? In the same way they learn their colours or numbers, by entering their learning sweet spot and soaking it all up like a sponge. It is, after all, just another code to crack.

Jesse has just in the last few months become interested in words and letters. He is noticing words that rhyme and is making up little limericks. He is asking me how to spell words and practicing his writing by making a comic book. He is pointing out words on billboards and asking me what they say. And we read books, a lot them.

I think this little learning curve may take a bit longer than learning his colours or even the numbers, but that's ok. After all, once he is in a learning sweet spot, I couldn't stop him if I tried! Especially with the dangling carrot of an uncompleted Harry Potter series.

AT THE BEGINNING
BY JAMIE BERG

I'm the mother of a four-year-old and I never thought I'd homeschool. Over time, and for our own reasons, we began to love the idea of it. So I researched and read and met with other families and read and Instagrammed and read, and now we plan. Because we have a preschool-aged kid, we really are at the beginning of it all.

The single greatest thing to remember going in is that it's all about priorities. So it is with life, so it is with homeschooling. Your priorities will guide you, shape your days, recenter you when you need it, and remind you why you're doing what you're doing. The starting of it can be a little overwhelming, so here are five questions for your beginning, to help you choose what priorities will be.

WHAT WOULD YOUR IDEAL LIFE LOOK LIKE?

A grand idea experiment, I know, but you're counterculture now! Choosing to homeschool pulls you outside of the mainstream life and frees you up to reconsider what your life could be. Would you travel more? Read a new book every week? Learn photography? Live off the land? Volunteer abroad? Make your own movies? And on and on. This is a fun conversation for the whole family to have, and it will give everyone an idea of what you wish for and value.

WHAT WOULD YOUR IDEAL DAY LOOK LIKE?

This question lets you narrow in a bit more on what you answered for the first. An ideal life is such a Big Concept, and it can be hard to wrap your mind around. An ideal day is easy to imagine.

You can think of this in broad terms: My ideal day would be to wake up early, make breakfast together as a family, play outside, build something together, cuddle on the couch with a book, and have an adventure before bedtime.

You can also use word association: My ideal day would have - Nature. Family. Art. Service. Big Ideas. Laughter. Sweets. Savories. Sharing. Adventure. Building. Dancing. Togetherness.

Or you could get super specific. However you choose to think about it, this question will help you better understand your priorities, which will help you shape your homeschooling days. It's good for each member of the family to answer this question, as it helps you understand everyone's rhythm, hopes, and priorities.

WHAT QUALITIES DO YOU HOPE TO DEVELOP AND INSTILL IN YOUR FAMILY?

As a homeschooling parent, you'll most likely have more time to personally direct and develop your child's moral compass and character. So which qualities are most important to you? Kindness? Curiosity? Resilience? Bravery? Joyfulness? Confidence? Patience? Compassion? Respect? Once you zone in on your top priorities in this area, you can find ways to practice those qualities in your home. This can guide you in choosing which books to read, for instance, or which projects to embark on, or even how to approach learning in your home.

WHAT SKILLS ARE IMPORTANT FOR YOU TO PRACTICE & DEVELOP IN YOUR CHILD?

You might have an instinctual answer to this question (i.e. reading and math skills). I find this is an area where outside knowledge can really help. Some find it enlightening to read about the Common Core Standards for the grades nearest their child just to have an idea of what other children his age might be learning in traditional school. That can offer background knowledge and a potential foundation to build from.

Other families connect with a certain style of teaching - Montessori, Unschooling, Classical, etc - which will most likely align with their style of parenting. They then find books that explore those philosophies deeper, or curriculum that follows their chosen philosophy, and use these to decide which skills to teach when.

WHAT PEOPLE AND ORGANIZATIONS WOULD SUPPORT YOU AND YOUR FAMILY IN YOUR SCHOOLING?

Though the responsibility of your child's education is with you, keep yourself mindful of the village. Not only will your child often benefit from other teachers and teammates, you will too. You can find support there, or a respite, or a community. So educate yourself on your options.

What classes does your community center offer? Ours offers a Tennis program and my kid loves it. Are there specialty schools nearby? We take a Spanish Class at a local language center, as well as a Nature Class through a local nature school. Are there local family or homeschooling groups you could join for support? Our area has a MOMS Group and few Wild + Free communities not too far away, both of which we've tried.

If your child shows an interest in something, know what your options are and seek out a way to try it. At the age of four, my son has tried art class, ballet, horse-riding, and soccer, as well as the aforementioned tennis, spanish, and nature classes. He also spent time in a Montessori summer program. We've been to children's theaters and a multitude of museums. And we've been able to do all of these things because I educated myself on what our local resources are.

For some people, the luckiest among us I think, family and friends prove to be priceless in their support. If you're able, lean into them.

ISSUE ONE | SECULAR HOMESCHOOLER

MATH BEYOND WORKSHEETS
BY E.M. STONE

I'm probably not alone when I say that math was my least favorite subject while growing up. Unfortunately I never gave it a proper chance and I assumed because most of the people around me dreaded it that there was no chance I'd ever learn to appreciate it. I also can't help but think "Ha ha, Ms. Goninske!" every time I pull out my phone calculator wherever I happen to need it.

Now I homeschool and while we are mostly of the unschooling philosophy, I enforce math studies on daily basis. It's like veggies, I guess. When you start adulting you realize that math and veggies are important. At first it was exciting to pick one out of four-hundred-billion possible mathematics programs. You make your selection. You order you kit and book. You watch the videos. You laminate a bunch of things for the sheer joy of melting plastic to paper. You watch your child progress and then everyone gets bored and doesn't want to do it anymore. That's how it went here. I wondered if math was doomed to be boring for everyone forever. This is homeschooling! We're supposed to be able to do things differently. Why am I sitting my child at a desk with worksheets and calling that a complete subject study?

In an attempt to spend less time in a workbook and more time in the real world, here are some ideas to get you started:

MATH MATH A PART OF GAME NIGHT:

My second-born first learned how to count by playing Uno. She probably knew basics beforehand but Uno is where she solidified her knowledge of what the number shapes actually look like and how to match them to one another. (Hint: it helps with color recognition as well.) The biggest way it helped was to teach her how to differentiate between 6 and 9. It's like an adrenaline-pumped $7 tutor.

Other math games that totally rock are Clumsy Thief in the Candy Shop (for counting to 20), Clumsy Thief (for counting to 100), and Zeus on the Loose (also for counting to 100). There are so many games you can play with just a simple set of dice or a standard playing deck. Our deck is Hogwarts themed.

MAKE MUFFINS WITH MATH:

Fractions are a weird concept to grasp. I still have issues myself but have been learning so much from helping my kids understand them. One thing I like to do is to set them up to bake muffins or cookies but take away the one-cup measuring devices. So not only are they measuring out ¼ cup sugar and ⅓ cup oil but they're also having to use the ½ cup measurement twice to get their 1 cup of flour. They're figuring out how to add fractions and I've barely had to show them anything. I really believe that the combination of touch, taste, and smells during the baking experience will help solidify natural mathematic concepts in their noggin better than worksheets will. Another baking-themed math activity that we did was to paint paper plates to look like a pumpkin pie. Then I cut it into 8 parts and wrote the fraction size on each piece so they could have fun adding the pie slices together to try and make bigger fraction sizes!

DO ART THAT'S SECRETLY MATH:

Sometimes we forget that math is more than 1+1. It's also shapes and spirals and negative space and positive space. You can make parabolic curves using straight lines with a ruler or create tangrams out of colorful paper and see how many scenes you can arrange. During my 2D Design course in college we were assigned this exact project as homework. Little did I know it wouldn't be a chore because my oldest stayed up with me late into the night playing with the tangram cuts and gluing them to poster boards. The objective was to make one scene with a full tangram set, but no more or less than that. We ended up making a sad, but awesome, picture depicting a fox attacking a mama rabbit that was defending her baby rabbit.

Another math art project idea is to cut out construction paper circles based on the Fibonacci sequence and arrange those into different scenes. If you have a lot of yarn sitting around then pop some nails into an embroidery hoop and spend hours playing with your new multiplication circle!

"We encourage children to read for enjoyment, yet we never encourage them to do 'math' for enjoyment."

Rachel McAnallen

UTILIZE MATH IN TECHNOLOGY:

Technology is not the enemy. In fact, computer games and apps can be some of the most exciting ways to learn mathematical concepts. They're fun, they're exciting, and often involve strategy. When I was a child I learned how to code completely through my addiction to Neopets.com. My parents were wary of the internet and its dangers but supported my exploration regardless. I came alive learning Neopoint currency strategy as well as designing and coding my own guilds from scratch to increase my currency opportunities. I spent entire summers on this site. Now as an adult I can design and code a website, I know how to run an online community, I understand the nature of the online world combined with money management, and I know a scam when I see one. (I was duped out of my hard-earned 100,000 Neopoints one time in an attempt to buy a rare PetPet from a shady dealer. A harsh lesson learned in a safe way.) I never took a class on any of these things. I never learned them in public school. I learned and absorbed all of this through online fun.

TURN NATURE WALKS INTO MATH STUDY:

Alright nature junkies, I'm looking at you. Use your nature hikes to count mushrooms or create patterns out of leaves, pinecones, and rocks. Take photos for your portfolio proof! Look for naturally occuring symmetry and create symmetry by building a gigantic nature mandala. Discover the age of a tree. Count the leaves on a stem. How many stones can you stack before the pile falls over?

MONEY MANAGEMENT IS A VITAL SKILL... AND ALSO MATH!

If kids don't learn money management before they hit the real world, they're screwed until they learn through mistakes. It's so much better that they learn while at home and with smaller quantities of money. The most exciting part of this endeavor? It's math! At home we've started offering an allowance on a weekly basis based on our children's ages. We have pretend bills and coins from Toys R Us (R.I.P.) that we use to pay them with, while their actual cash is on a kid-friendly debit card called Greenlight. The pretend money helps by giving them a tangible visual to count and divide into their spend-save-share jars. They have a ledger that they keep everything written in. When they make a debit card purchase, they write changes to their accounts into their ledger and then hand over the correct amount of "cash" once we're at home. We opt for the debit card instead of just giving them actual cash because I'm a germaphobe and card junkie. I wish it were a much more philosophical reason. If we didn't do the fake cash, they'd never actually learn what a dollar bill looks like and my youngest would lose interest and assume that money is an invisible thing in the air. This way they learn the way we did as kids but can eventually grow out of the cash and switch to solely using a debit card.

> **LIKE THESE IDEAS AND WANT MORE? EXPLORE ONLINE, AND WHEN IN DOUBT CONSULT YOUR BEST FRIEND, PINTEREST.**

FINDING FREEDOM WITH MINIMALISM
BY LINDSAY RICE

I found minimalism out of necessity. I was homeschooling my oldest, trying to keep my wild and adventurous toddler occupied, and coping with a very colicky baby, add a small business and a large house to keep clean into the mix and I was stretched way past my breaking point. I was up late one night scrolling through articles about how to juggle motherhood and life, soaking up all the advice of other moms hoping something would make sense to me. That is how I came across minimalism.

Article after article promised an easier to manage life, more engaged children, anxiety and stress lifted from tired shoulders. I was sold. I began to go through my house one room at a time and slowly adopted a minimalist lifestyle. It turns out all of those writers and bloggers that touted minimalism as the best thing ever knew what they were talking about.

We are about to take our minimalism journey to the next level as we build a tiny house for our family of six (five humans and a fur baby), but minimalism doesn't have to go to that level. It can simply mean getting rid of excess. Before embracing this lifestyle I was a curriculum hoarder. I had tools and manipulatives from my days as a public school teacher and piles of workbooks I was sure I might use one day, even though we rarely use workbooks. This habit left me feeling so overwhelmed with school - too many different curriculums to fit into our school year, so many subjects and projects, my anxiety flared every time I walked into our school room.

After pairing down our school room, and ending up with a school cart, I find planning and getting ready for our school day easier than ever. I have kept only the essentials, and we still follow a reading and math curriculum that fits our family well, but outside of those two subjects we don't have an endless supply of materials or workbooks to wade through. We read a lot, and books take up a decent amount of space so we utilize the library instead of purchasing all of our books and having to find storage, we also trade with other homeschooling families.

The first step to simplifying is to look at what you use everyday and set it aside, then go through the rest and make a pile of items that haven't been used in three months. This can be hard at first, people tend to develop an attachment to their things, and rightfully so. You worked hard to purchase the items in your possession! Once those items become overwhelming though, it is ok to allow yourself to let go without the guilt. The freedom of having less is so worth it.

WHY THERE IS NO REQUIRED READING IN OUR HOMESCHOOL

BY HEATHER ESTERDAY

Recently, I picked up *Death Comes to the Archbishop* by Willa Cather, along with a few other titles, from the library. I intentionally grabbed several novels, as I had convinced myself that I wouldn't like the Cather novel. Why? Because in high school my best friend was required to read My Antonia, also by Cather, and hated it. She complained about it so frequently and vehemently that twenty-five years later, I still believed that I wouldn't like Cather's (highly acclaimed) work.

But I do. At forty-five, I enjoy Cather's rich language and vivid descriptions of the Southwest, where I have traveled extensively and made my home. Historical fiction is now my favorite genre. This got me thinking: Would I have liked *Death Comes to the Archbishop* in high school? In college? I don't think I would have. My tastes have changed, matured. Books have seasons in our lives, and I was not ready for this one before now.

We are a family that enjoys great literature regularly. But I don't have, and never plan to have, a required reading list for my kids. Much of the literature that I was assigned to read in school I didn't enjoy, and I actually came to loathe some of it (I'm looking at you, *The Great Gatsby*). I know from experience that being required to read a book can ruin the experience of that book (and even that author) irreparably. I recently re-read Gatsby, and sadly, I still feel that way. A book that we may not be ready for yet could in the future become a favorite - unless we ruin it with a forced slog through a novel you can't relate to and don't enjoy.

Some may suggest that if we don't make children read certain books, they won't choose harder titles on their own, and won't learn to deal with slower pacing, complex storylines and difficult vocabulary. I can only offer up our family's experience as reassurance. We read aloud a lot. We read a wide variety of genres, including graphic novels, amazing picture books, non-fiction, easy readers, and a lot of "children's literature" and "classics." None of it is ever required. If we start a book, and we're just not into it, we stop. We recently did this with *The Rescuers*. We tried, and it just wasn't engaging for us. Perhaps it was the slow pacing or how dated it was – but we have also enjoyed other novels that were slow paced and dated, most recently, *Homer Price* and *Ginger Pye*. I confess that I kept asking my kids if they wanted to stop reading *Ginger Pye* because the slow pace was driving me nuts! They said no.

Another reason why we don't have a list of required reading is that great literature is not a monolith. When we get wrapped up in ticking all the boxes and making sure we read all the books on the list, we forget that these lists are made by people. People with opinions. And opinions vary as to what should be included as "great literature."

Much of the English literary canon excludes authors of color, authors from other cultures, and LGBTQ authors. Book lists have been doing a better job at including diverse voices on their must-read lists, but the numbers are still paltry. The New York Public Library's list has 25 out of their top 100 children's books featuring characters that are not white. Time Magazine's list has nine, and School Library Journal has only five – out of 100. Many of the lists also don't yet include recent titles that are fantastic, such as Peter Brown's *The Wild Robot* and Sara Pennypacker's *Pax*.

In addition to not requiring my kids to read certain books, I don't police what they choose to read. Even though we are both Charlotte Mason influenced and very book-centric in our approach, I let my kids read "twaddle" - and I don't label it that or make judgments about it. I let them read whatever brings them joy. My older son basically learned to read from graphic novels, and I hear that from other parents frequently. Am I going to point out *Captain Underpants* at the library? No. Am I going to stop them from reading it? Also no.

My kids, when left to their own devices, first choose books like *Narwhal and Jelly*, *The Bad Guys*, Minecraft novels, and Minecraft and Lego How-To guides. But my nine-year old has also read his way through more book series that I can remember, although nobody would claim that *The Magic Tree House* or *Geronimo Stilton* are great literature. Their choices haven't in any way dampened their enthusiasm for, or understanding of, classics like *The Wizard of Oz*, *James and the Giant Peach*, *The Complete Polly and the Wolf*, *The Miraculous Journey of Edward Tulane*, *The Family Under the Bridge*, and *Where the Mountain Meets the Moon*.

My parents owned a liquor store for many years, and my dad was very knowledgeable about wine. He once told me that people would often come in wanting to purchase "a good wine." They were hyper-focused on picking the "correct" wine, so they would ask him for help. He would often remind them, "A good wine is one you like."

Shouldn't reading be about pleasure too? A good book is one you like. It doesn't mean that they won't enjoy more difficult titles later. A 2015 study by Scholastic showed a 10% decline over five years in the number of kids reading for pleasure. Most of us have seen the dismal statistics that one-third of high school graduates, and 42% of college graduates never read another book for the rest of their lives after graduating.

In our homeschool, we take the long view when it comes to literature selection. My only literary goal is to make sure that my kids love to read, regardless of what they are reading, because a love of reading creates life-long readers and learners.

SOURCES:
1. nypl.org/childrens100
2. time.com/100-best-childrens-books
3. listchallenges.com/top-100-childrens-novels
4. scholastic.com/readingreport/key-findings.htm

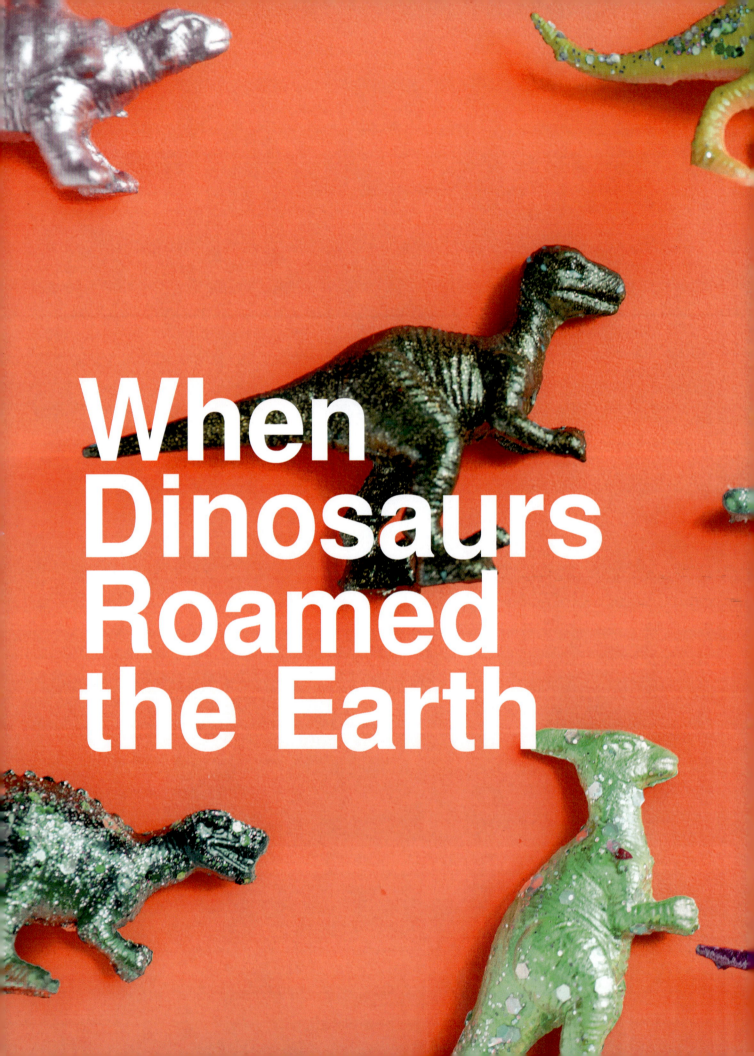

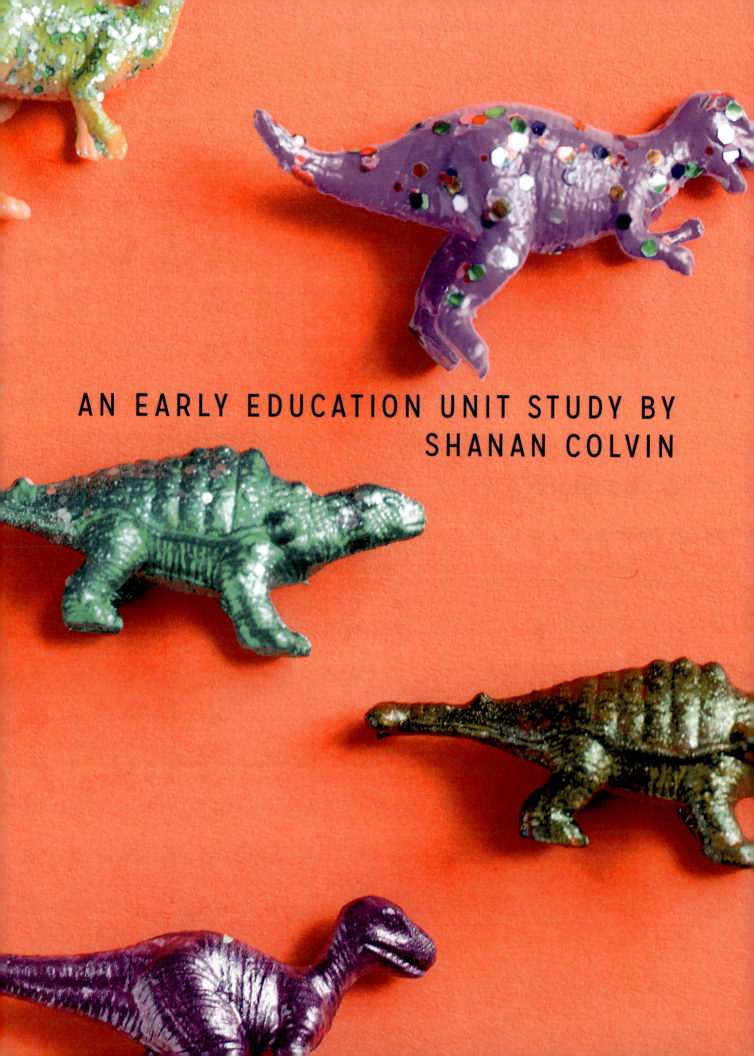

AN EARLY EDUCATION UNIT STUDY BY
SHANAN COLVIN

GOALS/OBJECTIVES:

Learn about the age of the dinosaurs and the tools paleontologists use to study them.

VOCABULARY & SPELLING:

Dinosaur, Era, Mesozoic, Triassic, Jurassic, Cretaceous, Paleontology, Paleontologist, Shovel, Chisel, Brush, Knife, Hammer, Sedimentary Rock, Sandstone, Limestone, Bones, & Skeleton.

LITERATURE READ-ALOUDS:

How Do Dinosaurs Eat Their Food by Janet Yolen Literature

The Usborne Big Book of Dinosaur by Alex Frith and Fabiano Fiorin

Lift-the-Flap Questions and Answers About Dinosaurs by Katie Daynes and Marie-Eve Tremblay

Dinosaurs Before Dark by Mary Pope Osborne

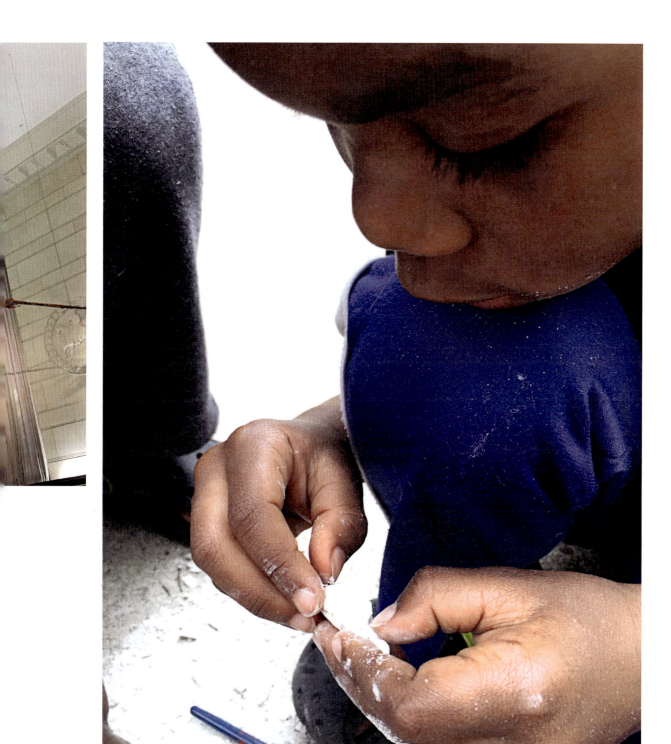

ACTIVITIES:

ACTIVITY: Play-Doh Fossils & Imprints

MATERIALS: Playdough, leaves, plastic dinosaurs, shells, rocks, etc.

PROCEDURE: Make impressions in your Play-Doh and discuss the formation of fossil casts and molds. If you make the impressions ahead of time, your kiddos can be paleontologists and try to identify which objects created which impressions.

ACTIVITY: Dino Dig Backyard Fun

MATERIALS: Dirt or sand, rocks, shells, plastic dinosaurs, shovels, and old paintbrushes.

PROCEDURE: Hide your geological treasures in your sandbox and let the kids dig away! Use the paint brushes to clean the debris off their discoveries.

ACTIVITY: Sand Art Timeline

MATERIALS: Clear plastic bottle with lid, small funnel, plastic Ziplock bags, salt, and food coloring.

PROCEDURE: Make three different "sand" colors by putting desired amount of salt and food coloring into separate plastic baggies. Mix them together and then leave open to dry out. Determine the length of the Jurassic, Triassic, and Cretaceous time periods. Pour different "sand" colors into the plastic bottle to make a visual timeline.

VISIT MUSEUMSUSA.ORG TO SEARCH FOR GREAT FIELD TRIP OPPORTUNITIES NEAR YOU!

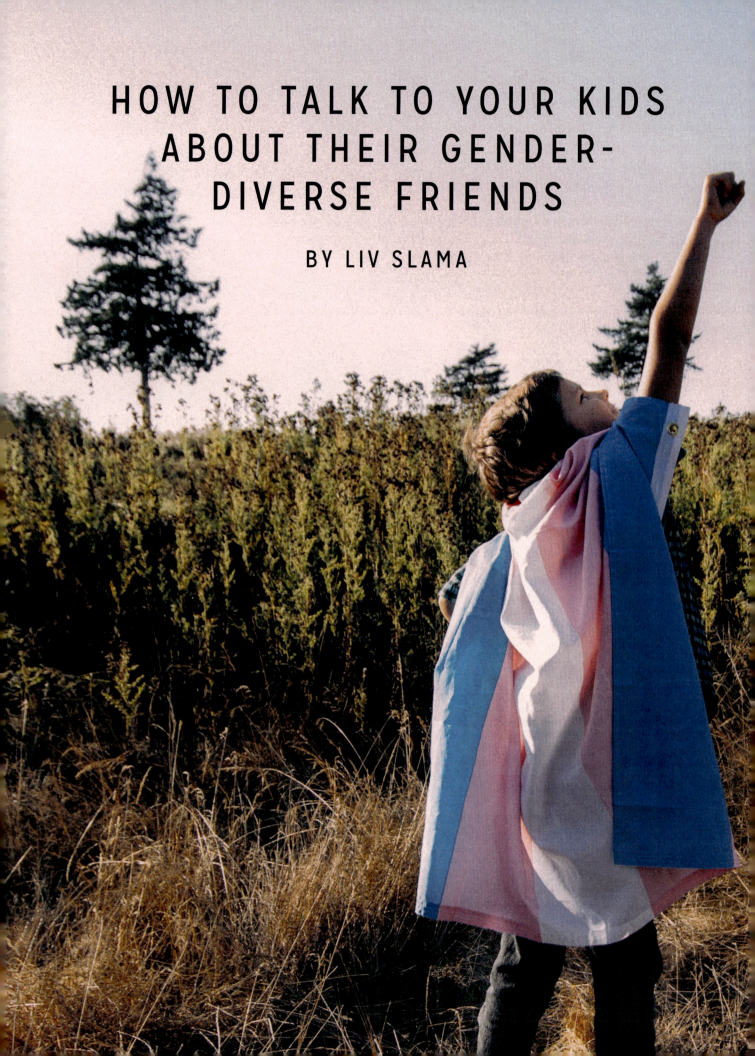

HOW TO TALK TO YOUR KIDS ABOUT THEIR GENDER-DIVERSE FRIENDS

BY LIV SLAMA

We were waiting for the bus to take us home from school. Luke's preschool center was on my community college campus, so every day that year we made the trek to and from school together. After a full day of classes, the ride home was usually a quiet one. Luke would snack at the bus stop and snuggle into me. He would tell me bits and pieces about his day while I half-listened, half-scrolled through my emails and Instagram photos.

"BUT WHY DO MY FRIENDS AND TEACHERS KEEP CALLING ME A GIRL WHEN I TOLD THEM I'M A BOY?"

That got my attention. I put my phone down. We'd had conversations about his gender before, and on more than one occasion he had told me he was a boy. But at three-and-a-half, I'd assumed he didn't really know what he was talking about. When pressed, his only explanation was the word "boy" "just felt better." Each time, I would smile and tell him he could be whatever he wanted to be, and wouldn't think much more about it.

This time, I stopped and listened. He had been consistently, persistently telling me he was a boy, and now he was frustrated the people around him weren't listening. Over the course of the next few months, Luke cut his hair, picked out some new clothes he felt more comfortable in, and asked us to use he/him pronouns. He was totally socially transitioned by the middle of his second year of preschool.

Three years later, Luke is one of the happiest, healthiest kids you'll meet. Most of the time, he presents himself in a stereotypically "masculine" way. He prefers short haircuts, loose, comfortable pants and tee shirts, and likes his shoes to be as practical and worn-in as as possible. When he goes in public, he easily passes as a cisgender little boy. This isn't the case for some of his gender-nonconforming and intersex friends. Even in our progressive little pocket of the Pacific Northwest, people aren't always sure what to do with visibly gender-nonconforming people.

Gender is a spectrum, but many of us have no idea how to talk to our kids about that spectrum. Often this is because we are comfortably cisgender, and the idea that gender is anything other than binary is still a new concept to us. Sometimes, we simply don't have the language to express what we've known to be true for years.

These barriers shouldn't prevent us from having these conversations with our kids. It's important to have these conversations because (1) giving children this language at an early age allows them to introspect about their own gender identity, and (2) they are going to be interacting with gender-diverse people for the rest of their lives. It's important they understand how to include transgender, gender-nonconforming, and intersex people in their language and their world.

TALK ABOUT IT AS EARLY AS YOU CAN.

Just like with everything else, the earlier to start taking to your kids about gender identity, the deeper their understanding will be. If you can begin having these conversations before too many gender-based stereotypes have been introduced, you can avoid having to undo all of the thinking you yourself are working to overcome.

Not only that, studies have shown young children's ability to pick up on language far exceeds that of adults. A great example of this is how difficult it is for an adult to integrate the gender-neutral "they" into their vocabulary, despite being otherwise supportive of the gender-diverse people in their life. Once you are in the habit of using compulsively gendered language, it can be hard to break yourself of it. If you can avoid creating those discriminatory boxes within your child's language in the first place, your child will have an easier time understanding the gender spectrum going forward.

LEAD BY EXAMPLE.

The best way to teach your children how to use inclusive language is to model it for them. If you don't know where to start, remember to only bite off one piece at a time. Identify the speech habits you want change, and intentionally focus on them one at a time.

If you find yourself frequently addressing groups of people with "Ladies and Gentlemen" or "Guys," spend a month retraining your brain to reach for more inclusive catch-all greetings, such as "folks" or "ya'll." Once you've got that down, consider eliminating "gender-guesses" from your vocabulary altogether by referring to anyone who hasn't specifically told you how they identify as "they." This one takes a while and is something you have to be intentional about, but it's a great way to avoid misgendering someone from the get-go.

LET THEM STEER THE CONVERSATIONS.

This has been the single most effective way I have found to have conversations about gender with my kids. While this stuff comes naturally to Luke, his sister struggles a bit more. She gleefully identifies as a cisgender girl, and the nuances of the gender spectrum often evade her.

Asking your kids to back up their assertions is a great way to turn the conversation around and get them to think about what they're saying. Ask questions like, "How do you know?" and "Have you talked to them about it?" This reinforces that you can't know what a person's gender is by looking at them.

RELAX.

Learning a new way to communicate can be overwhelming, and putting it into practice can be even more stressful. It took me six months to stop misgendering my kid, and even then, I didn't always know the best way to communicate with other people about his gender identity. It felt— and often still feels— like I was rewiring my brain. But as my child's first and most passionate advocate, I never stopped learning and trying to do better. Eventually, the conversations about gender flowed more naturally.

It feels clunky at first, but with practice, the language comes more easily. Undoubtedly, your kids will pick up on it before you do. In every instance I've witnessed, kids who are asked to adapt their language to be more inclusive are able to do so immediately and seamlessly.

Whatever you do, don't wait until you feel completely ready to talk about gender diversity with your kids. Share what you've learned, and see what they have to say. Some of my biggest breakthroughs on the subject were had while talking about gender with my son. Give them the language, and follow their lead.

ISSUE ONE

Thanks For Your Support & Connection

CONTRUBUTE TO FUTURE ISSUES:
SecularHomeschooler.com/Contribute

DISCOVER SECULAR RESOURCES ON AMAZON:
Amazon.com/Shop/SecularHomeschooler

SEARCH OUR WORLD-WIDE RESOURCE DATABASE:
SecularHomeschooler.com/Secular-Homeschool-Guide

FACEBOOK.COM/
SECULARHOMESCHOOLER

INSTAGRAM.COM/
SECULARHOMESCHOOLER

Photography Credits: Victoria Gamlen Photography (Cover), Nathan Dumlao (10), Annie Spratt (pages 12, 37, 54, 66, 86, 89), Aidan Kahng (16), Brandi Redd (22), E.M. Stone (57, 78, 81), Vlad Tchompalov (38), Will Swann (42), Dean Rose (44), Josh Calabrese (51), Samual Zeller (62), Tong Nyugen Van (74), Romina Veliz (76-77), Liv Slama (96-97, 101), Anwulika Anigbo (103).

Made in the USA
Lexington, KY
15 September 2018